365 ways to Say
"I LOVE YOU"
to Your Kids

JAY PAYLEITNER

HARVEST HOUSE PUBLISHERS

EUGENE, OREGON

Cover by e210 Design, Eagan, Minnesota

Cover photo © iStockphoto / omgimages

Illustrations by Rex Bohn, Bohn Illustration, Geneva, Illinois; www.rexbohn.com

365 WAYS TO SAY "I LOVE YOU" TO YOUR KIDS
Copyright © 2011 by Jay K. Payleitner
Published by Harvest House Publishers
Eugene, Oregon 97402
www.harvesthousepublishers.com

ISBN 978-0-7369-4473-1 (paperback)
ISBN 978-0-7369-4474-8 (eBook)

Printed in the United States of America

11 12 13 14 15 16 17 18 19 / BP-SK / 10 9 8 7 6 5 4 3 2 1

For Mom and Dad,
who taught me how to love.

Love Is a Verb

The best way to say "I love you" to your kids is out loud. They need to hear it early and often. Babies need to hear it. Third-graders need to hear it. Teenagers especially need to hear it. Hey, even parents still like to hear it from *their* parents. Right?

But spoken words are just one way to express how much you love your kids.

Love is a verb. The act of demonstrating love to your children yields great dividends. It models. It teaches. It affirms. Mom and Dad, you are loving your children every time you console, inspire, equip, rescue, or challenge them. Love sacrifices, disciplines, and protects. Love delights. Love gets both silly and solemn. As the Bible says, "Love never fails."

You may already own several books that provide scholarly theoretical doctrine on optimal parenting strategies. But you won't find any of that nonsense here.

Nope. This book comes right out and tells you what to do. Three hundred sixty-five times. If you implement just a handful of these ideas, you are headed in the right direction and this book is worth every nickel you paid for it. (If it was a gift, you're way ahead of the game.)

So how can you use this book to start saying "I love you" to your kids? It couldn't be easier. Simply place the book on your desk, workbench, counter, toilet tank, or nightstand and open it at random whenever you get the chance. When an idea strikes your fancy, go for it.

You see, *becoming* a parent is biology. But *being* a parent is not a science at all. It's about unexpected discoveries, sweet serendipitous moments, heart-wrenching confrontations, breathless bouts of confusion, and quiet soul-satisfying triumphs.

Mostly parenting is about just being there and showing your kids you love them somehow every single day.

Saying "I Love You" Every Day

1.

Carry one or two photos of each
of your kids in your wallet.

2.

Carry hundreds of photos in your iPod.

3.

Let them push the buttons in the elevator.

4.

Get a heart-shaped cookie cutter and use
it for lunch meat, pancakes, French toast,
sandwiches, and sometimes even cookies!

5.

Share inside jokes.

6.

For no reason at all, offer to do the dishes
when it's their turn at the sink.

7.

Tell your kids something you struggled
with when you were their age.

8.

Patiently explain Sunday morning funnies
when they don't get the joke.

9.

Quit smoking.

10.

Kneel in front of your three-year-old to tie their shoes.

11.

Toss Wiffle® balls to your four-year-old (aiming very
carefully to hit their huge fat red bat as they swing).

12.

Refrain from yelling at referees
when they clearly blow a call.

13.

Do noisy cheek kisses.

14.

Watch their favorite television program with them. (Without making fun of the bad acting, predictable script, or ridiculous plot.)

15.

Learn the international sign language for "I love you" and use it across the room, across the yard, or across the gym.

16.

Keep a secret hidden stash of colored markers and poster boards. When they remember that homework assignment at nine o'clock the night before it's due, you are the hero of the realm.

17.

Make a big deal about an improvement in a report card. (Don't say "It's about time," or spoil the celebration by pointing out other grades that could also improve.)

18.

Inspect the lawn after they've finished mowing and find more good things than bad things.

19.

Let them name the family pet. (This encourages creativity.)

20.

Let them feed the family pet. (This encourages responsibility.)

21.

Give sincere compliments. (Even if their outfit is nontraditional, their musicianship is dreadful, or their grammar is horrible, find *something* to compliment with honesty and sincerity.)

22.

Share silly secrets.

23.

When you think of them for some reason during the day, send a text, tweet, or e-mail with short, specific details.

24.

Go for a walk. Hold hands. Skip.

25.

When your kid gets behind the wheel of a car and heads off on an excursion longer than three blocks, speak this phrase: "Love you. Drive careful."

26.

When your kid gets into someone else's car, speak this phrase to the driver: "Drive careful. Precious cargo."

27.

Here's a great line you might use with your kids every day: "What are we celebrating today?" Chances of getting a thoughtful response skyrocket compared to "How you doing?" or "How was school today?"

28.

Skip rocks on a pond or river. Celebrate six or more *kerplunk*s. Agonize dramatically over a mere four or five *kerplunk*s. Groan over two or three *kerplunk*s. Mock single *kerplunk*s.

29.

Teach them how to play chess or checkers. But don't let them win.

30.

Ask them to teach you how to play their favorite video game. Try to win. (Don't worry, you won't!)

31.

Watch an old Frank Capra movie together, like *It's a Wonderful Life, Meet John Doe, It Happened One Night,* or *Mr. Smith Goes to Washington.*

32.

Watch a more recent feel-good movie that isn't filled with sex and violence and the entire family can enjoy together, like *Breaking Away*, *That Thing You Do*, *Ferris Bueller's Day Off*, or *Groundhog Day*.

33.

Drag them out of bed to see a lunar eclipse.

34.

Call them out on the front lawn to see a double rainbow.

35.

Rake leaves together.

36.

Stop raking when a "V" of geese flies over, headed north for the winter. Explain that scientists still aren't sure why they fly like that. It could be to reduce air resistance. Or it could be for navigation. By the way, that "V" is called an echelon.

37.

Take their photo on the first day of school. Every year. Keep a small album reserved for those shots only. Flip through quickly and watch them grow right before your eyes!

38.

Surf the Internet until you find a cool, appropriate website that relates to their favorite team, musical group, school subject, author, TV show, etc. Send them a link to the site with a short note.

39.

Make sure they know they can call you for anything at any time, no matter what. That's any time for any reason. Then, when you see your kid's name on the caller ID, stop what you're doing and pick up the phone or, at the very least, call back ASAP.

40.

Ceremoniously present them with a cell phone, explaining that it's really all about keeping lines of communication open between you and them.

41.

Build a snowman. A classic one with carrot nose, charcoal eyes, and scarf. Or a wacky one with tentacles, horns, a tail, a hollow belly, paper plate ears, and a hula skirt.

42.

Make fruit smoothies for everyone. (In a blender mix crushed ice, milk, orange juice, a banana, a can of peaches, a few strawberries, peeled apple slices, and a scoop or two of vanilla ice cream. Or any combination.)

43.

Take a trip to the batting cage before their baseball or softball tryouts, or before a big game.

44.

Do cool things as an entire family.

45.

Do cool things one kid at a time.

46.

Do cool things with the entire family including your kids' grandparents.

47.

Make an extra effort—but don't be too obvious—
to give a word of encouragement or be a listening
ear to any of your children's friends who may
be going through a tough family situation.

48.

Apologize when you mess up.

49.

Start a tradition. (Kids love traditions.)

50.

Say "I love you" and then add a wink.

51.

Help them choose a musical instrument.

52.

Be patient and encouraging when they practice
their music. (Especially if it's the clarinet.)

53.

Don't make empty threats. Think before you make an ultimatum, because if you threaten "No TV for a week," you need to be prepared to follow through. If you say, "One more whine and we are leaving this store" and there is one more whine—leave that store immediately!

54.

Go bird-watching armed with a full-color bird book. Let them be in charge of the identification process.

55.

Sometimes be the only parent in the stands at a sporting event. (Even if bad weather, time of day, distance from home, or general parent apathy keeps everyone else away, your child still wants you there.)

56.

Give piggyback rides.

57.

To a three-year-old don't say, "Do you want to eat your sandwich?" Say, "Eat your sandwich."

58.

Examine a spiderweb with them.

59.

Spend an afternoon making sock puppets complete with button eyes, wild yarn hair, and red stitched-on lips.

60.

Pull a pair of warm sweat socks out of the dryer, slide them on your hands, and have them chat with each other. Instant sock puppets!

61.

Sometimes, tell your kids "no."

62.

Sometimes rescue them. (When they've given it
their absolute best and done everything they can.)

63.

Sometimes *don't* rescue them. (When it's not
life threatening. Because we often learn more
from our failures than from our successes.)

Saying "I Love You" When You're in the Car

64.

Make sure everyone in the car is wearing a
seat belt. Don't make a game of it. Don't
say, "The car won't start unless the seat belts are
fastened." (That's a lie they'll figure out soon
enough.) Just say, "Seat belts!" And that's that.

65.

When they ask a question or state an opinion, turn
off the radio so you can give them your full attention.

66.

Unexpectedly stop for ice cream.

67.

Unexpectedly stop at a pet store. (Just to pet
the pets, not necessarily to buy the pets.)

68.

Don't curse infant car seats. Yes, they were
designed by government-appointed vehicular
terrorists. But remember that babies can pick
up on your tone and older siblings can pick
up on your choice of unsavory words.

69.

You know how sometimes when you're driving
you reach back and blindly swat at your kids for
misbehaving? Well, next time you're driving do just
the opposite. Reach your hand back over the seat and
give their eager hands or knobby knees a love squeeze.

70.

Volunteer to drive the carpool to practices,
games, and youth events. Listen to the
conversations in the backseat—and learn.

Saying "I Love You" Using Words

71.

"You make me smile."

72.

"I am so proud of you."

73.

"Where did you learn to do that? That's fantastic."

74.

"I look around and can't believe how
lucky I am to be part of this family."

75.

"You are a gift from God."

76.

"You're amazing."

77.

"You did that! That's epic."

78.

"Well played."

79.

"You probably don't even realize how much
your little brother looks up to you."

80.

"Hey, what's the biggest thing on
your mind right now?"

81.

"Hey sweetheart, come over here
and tell me about your day."

82.

"Hey big guy, come over here and
tell me about your day."

83.

"If they lined up all the eight-year-old girls
in the entire world, I'd choose you."*

---

* Idea borrowed from speaker and author John Trent.

84.

"You are just about the best thing
that ever happened to me!"

85.

"I'm sorry. You were right. I was
wrong. Will you forgive me?"

86.

When they don't make the team: "I'm so sorry.
I know you would have been awesome."

87.

When they don't make the cast list: "I'm
so sorry. I hurt for you."

88.

When their artwork isn't chosen: "I'm so
sorry. I know how hard you worked on it."

89.

"That's a great idea. I wish I had thought of it."

90.

"I was thinking about you all day today."

91.

"How did that geography quiz go?"

92.

"You know what? I love you."

93.

Say "I love you" without any conditions.
It's not "I love you when..." or "I love you
because..." or "I love you, but..."

More Saying "I Love You" Every Day

94.

Make s'mores at a campfire. Or in
the fireplace. Or on the stove.

95.

Don't let them sass you.

96.

Identify each of your children's love language.
(Read *The Five Love Languages* by Gary Chapman.)

97.

Give them more "do's" than "don'ts."

98.

Do dishes together. You wash. They dry. You chat.

99.

Talk about your family history.

100.

Have your kids make a family tree from memory. When they're done, add as much as you can. Then, ask older relatives to add a few more branches. If you're up for it, do some library or Internet research and see how far back you can go.

101.

Sometimes buy them candy at the grocery store checkout line and sometimes don't. (If you do it every time, it's no longer a special treat.)

102.

Mouth the words "I love you" without any sound at all.

103.

Don't let them quit a team, troop, club, or group when it gets tough, friends drop out, or they're not an instant success. Instead, help them see the big-picture benefits and set short-term goals.

104.

If they do end up quitting a team, give them a few days to process the loss. But then help them find something else that matches their gifts and passions.

105.

Despite well-intentioned warnings to the contrary, sometimes choose to live vicariously through your children. Maybe you never had the chance to ski, play football, practice archery, go to college, sing in public, play piano, parasail, climb a mountain, study medicine, or serve on a mission field. It's really okay to imagine your kids as an extension of yourself. Cheer them on. Share their passion. (In some cases, maybe it's not too late for you to join them!)

106.

Show them your school photos from junior high. Let them mock you.

107.
Cut an interesting article out of the paper that obviously pertains to one of their interests and leave it on the kitchen table.

108.
Be patient.

109.
Empower them to try new things.

110.
Find a good church. One that has programs for the season of life your kids are in. If you need guidance, check with neighborhood families who really seem to have their act together.

111.
Let them set their own alarm clock.

112.

During a visit to your parents, have your mom and dad tell your kids what you were like at their age.

113.

Build something out of wood. (A birdhouse, a bat house, a playhouse, a footstool, or just a board with lots of holes drilled through it.)

114.

Value their opinions.

115.

Spank them when they need to be spanked. Not out of frustration. Not often. Not when they're too young to get it. Not when they're older and it just doesn't work. Not in public. Definitely not if there's been any physical abuse in your family. Make sure they know what they did and why it was wrong. Hug them afterward. Also, make sure you and your spouse are in agreement on this issue. When in doubt, don't.

116.

Surprise them with new toothbrushes.
(Who doesn't love a new toothbrush?)

117.

Play practical jokes on your kids. Not
to embarrass or anger them, but just to
make them laugh at themselves.

118.

Insist they eat their vegetables.
(Don't make a big deal about it. Just insist.)

119.

Learn how to say "I love you" in
French: *Je t'aime [zhay-TEM]*.

120.

Learn how to say "I love you" in
Spanish: *Te quiero [tay-kee-AIR-oh]*.

121.

Learn how to say "I love you" in Italian:
Ti voglio bene [tee-VOLL-yo-BEN-ay].

122.

Learn how to say "I love you" in Russian:
Ya tebya liubliu [Ya te-BYA lyu-BLYU].

123.

Learn how to say "I love you" in
Pig Latin: *I-way uv-lay oo-yay*.

124.

Learn how to say "I love you" in German:
Ich liebe dich [EESH-LEE-buh-DEESH].

125.

Learn how to say "I love you" in Hawaiian:
Aloha wau ia 'oe [ah-LOW-ha VOW-ee-ah OH-ay].

126.

Learn how to say "I love you" in
Mandarin Chinese: *Wo ai ni [woe I nee]*.

127.

Learn how to say "I love you" in Gaelic:
Ta grá agam duit [TAH grah AHG um dwit].

128.

Learn how to say "I love you" in Morse code.
Instead of spelling out the entire eight letters, simply
tap out "88" which is Morse code shorthand for
"Love, hugs, and kisses to you." That's *dash-dot-
dot dash-dot-dot*. You can tap, snap, flash, whistle,
or blink that signal anytime or anywhere.

129.

Do a jigsaw puzzle. Let the youngest
puzzler put in the last piece!

130.

Inside a closet, behind a door, or on a bare stud
wall, mark the height of each of your kids. Include
their initials and the date. Repeat once per year
and make a point to promise you will always love
every inch of them. (Mark on a strip of wood or
plastic you can take with you when you move. Or
leave the measurements like ancient hieroglyphics
as proof your family grew on this site.)

131.

Instead of reading what it actually says on your
fortune cookie, say this: "Help! I'm a prisoner
in a Chinese bakery." See if they get the joke.

132.

Hang out at the library together. Make
it a once-a-month date.

133.

If possible, when it comes time to purchase your child something of real value (like a computer, bike, baseball bat, interview suit, camera, etc.), buy a really nice one, top-notch. Teach them how to care for it and help them see the value in being a good steward.

134.

Meet them halfway on some things. For example, if they have an impossible task (probably because of procrastination) but they are sincerely working hard on it, help them out.

135.

Play 20 Questions.

136.

Let them make bad decisions, but not *really* bad decisions.

137.

Encourage them to reach for the stars. To dream big dreams.

Saying "I Love You"
to Newborns

138.

Rub their tummy.

139.

Kiss their cheeks.

140.

Hold them. (It's really okay to leave
the car seat in the car!)

141.

Give them a first name that works (and doesn't
embarrass them) when they are 8, 18, and 38.

142.

Take lots of pictures. Even if it's kid number four.

143.

Have a fresh diaper and baby wipes within
arm's reach before you take off the old diaper.
Never leave them alone on a changing table.

144.

Get ready for the crazy crawling stage. Plug up the electrical outlets. Put safety latches on all the cabinets. Except one. (Let them pull out the shiny, noisy pots and pans.)

145.

Teach them how to love. Teach them how to be loved. That's the most important thing they learn in that first year of life.

146.

Swaddle. Get a swaddle blanket. Learn the swaddle fold. Sometimes called the "burrito wrap." (What seems confining to anyone over six months feels cozy and comfy to a newborn.)

Saying "I Love You" to Preschoolers

147.

As soon as your preschooler can spell a dozen
words (like "cat," "dog," "mom," "dad," "love," and
the names of family members) make a crossword
puzzle with all those words. Use sketches for clues.

148.

Take them to the park with the highest slide in town. Encourage, but don't push.

149.

Teach them how and when to dial 9-1-1.

150.

Be amazed when they bring you a bug, dandelion, or shiny rock.

151.

Get down on their level.

152.

The year before they enter kindergarten, give them a glimpse of the inside of their future school. Take them to a concert, play, or book fair of an older sibling or neighbor kid.

153.

Catch them in a lie. Make a big deal about it. Get nose to nose. Tell them softly how sad it makes you. Tell them you need to trust them. Make them feel rotten about it.*

---

* Idea borrowed from chapter 7, *52 Things Kids Need from a Dad*.

154.

Ask them to bring you a book to read. (If they bring you the same book four days in a row, go ahead and laugh about it, but read that book! Kids love repetition. They love to relive satisfying moments.)

155.

Make sure they know how much God loves them!

156.

Teach them the rock/paper/scissors hand game. (Know that small children *always* throw "scissors" on their first chance. If you want to delight them, you throw "paper." They win!)

157.

Let them make real, but not vital, decisions like which shirt to wear, which route to take to the mall, which fast-food restaurant to go to, which font to use on their birthday invitations, etc. Value their opinion and decision.

Saying "I Love You" to School-Age Kids

158.

Take them to an amusement park, but don't make fun of them for chickening out of the roller coaster.

159.

Put a Pez dispenser in their lunch.

160.

Be the Picture Lady volunteer for their classroom. (Even if you're a dad!)

161.

Dad, sign up to be a Watch D.O.G.S. (Dads of Great Students) volunteer at your kid's school. If they don't have a Watch D.O.G.S. program, start one! You'll be a hero to all the kids and families at your school.*

162.

Ask them for input on their preference for babysitter, but retain the right to hire whoever you want.

---

* Watch D.O.G.S. is a program of the National Center for Fathering, Fathers.com.

163.

Teach them something slightly difficult that their friends can't do. (Like how to juggle, recite the alphabet backward, recite all the United States presidents in eight seconds, do a few simple magic tricks, whistle with their fingers, or play the spoons.)

164.

Talk about when you were their age. Your fears. Your dreams. Your frustrations. Your successes.

165.

Climb a jungle gym with them.

166.

Climb a tree with them. Hang out on a comfortable branch.

167.

Challenge them to see who can make the best paper airplane. Judge each plane based on most time aloft, farthest distance traveled, creativity, and neatness.

168.

The first time your middle schooler forgets
their lunch, dutifully drive over and
hand deliver a bag lunch to school.

169.

The second time your middle schooler
forgets their lunch, let them go hungry (or
force them to mooch off their friends).

170.

Give them a few key office supplies they can
call their own and keep on their desk: scissors,
tape dispenser, calculator, and stapler. When
you need to borrow them, ask! And make
sure you return them when you're done.

171.

Teach a first- or second-grader the basics
of how to play a game that says, "For
ages 8 and older" on the box.

172.

In the summer, when they say, "There's nothing to do," give them some profitable ideas. Lemonade stand. Dog walking business. Dog washing business. Yard cleanup. Poop scooping.

173.

If they really get serious about a business, help them design business cards on your computer.

174.

Let them have a small part in a big household project.

175.

Let them sit on your lap any time they want, if they still want.

176.

Make stilts. This Saturday—together—research stilt designs, head to the lumber store, saw, drill, bolt, and walk tall. (Suddenly your eight-year-old is looking you in the eye.)

177.

Tuck them in every night.

Saying "I Love You"
to Teenagers

178.

Tuck them in most every night.

179.

Understand that the best way to show love
to a teenager is to prepare them for success
in the adult world. Help them develop
real world, big picture thinking.

180.

Make your home a place teens want to hang
out: a fridge full of soda pop, ice cream bars and
pizza in the freezer, a Ping-Pong table in the
basement, board games in the closet, and parents
(that's you) who are around but don't hover.

181.

Acknowledge their need for a few fashion
accoutrements that are completely different
than when you were a teenager. (Surprise!)

182.

Set and enforce a fairly early curfew.
(But willingly give an extra hour on special
request. That's what cell phones are for!)

183.

When you're in the passenger seat and they're behind
the wheel with a learner's permit in their back pocket,
tell them absolutely everything you can think of
when it comes to safe driving. If they snap at you, say
"Pull over." Then swap places and you drive home.

184.

Ceremoniously present them with their own set
of car keys. (And feel free to give another lengthy
safety/responsibility speech at the time.)

185.

Engage them in friendly debates about the best and/or the most influential movie directors, rock bands, children's authors, painters, explorers, and inventors. (Respect their point of view. Allow yourself to be swayed by well-presented evidence and thoughtful arguments.)

186.

Stick to your guns about moral issues.

187.

If they are having a busy and productive week, go ahead and do one of their big chores for them, like processing the laundry, mowing the lawn, cleaning the garage, vacuuming, etc.

188.

Let them paint their room. Patiently teach them about filling holes, surface preparation, removing switch plates, protecting the floor, the original purpose of masking tape, edging with a brush, minimizing drips, and smooth strokes with the roller. But don't criticize their inevitable mess ups. And, yes, let them pick their own color.

189.

Make sure they know you're not going to sleep at night until they come home and say "Good night."

190.

Dig out one of those silly games you enjoyed as a family ten years earlier: Ants in the Pants, Kerplunk™, Mouse Trap, Twister, Barrel of Monkeys.

191.

When ordering out, ask them what they want on the family pizza.

192.

Write "Love you" on a sticky note and
put it on their bathroom mirror.

193.

By their freshman year in high school, get them
talking about college. Junior year, take them
out of school for a day to visit a state university
and a smaller private college about two hours
away. Share their dreams. In the car, talk about
their gifts, strengths, dreams, and career goals.

194.

Volunteer your yard as the place for your teenager
and their friends to come for homecoming or prom
pictures. (Don't be upset if they go someplace else.)

195.

Take lots of homecoming and prom pictures. Use
a good camera. (Not one of those embarrassing
disposable cameras.) Surprise them when the dance
is over with photos back from one-hour photo
processing or printed out on your computer.

196.

Chaperone a high school dance. (But stay far, far away from your child. Amazingly, eventually they will come and say "hi" to you!)

197.

Slip your son or daughter an extra forty bucks as they leave for the school dance, especially if they're going to a fancy restaurant. The bill is always larger than they think.

198.

Maintain a constant supply of chips and salsa. (Invest in chips and salsa stock.)

199.

On a good day, when your younger teenager does something demonstrating a new maturity, pull out your Bible and show them 1 Corinthians 13:11-12: "When I was a child, I spoke and thought and reasoned as a child. But when I grew up, I put away childish things. Now we see things imperfectly as in a cloudy mirror, but then we will see everything with perfect clarity. All that I know now is partial and incomplete, but then I will know everything completely, just as God now knows me completely" (NLT). Congratulate them on taking on new, grown-up perspectives and responsibilities. Remind them that all adults—including you—still have much to learn.

200.

Make sure they know how to tip.

201.

Make sure they know about automatic gratuities added to the bill for parties of six or more, and that they don't really need to tip any more than that!

202.

Respectfully ask questions about the music they listen to so that you can understand it better. (And understand *them* better.)

203.

Pull out some of your favorite old albums and dust off the old turntable or cassette player. Chances are your teen already knows the lyrics.

Saying "I Love You" to Young Adults

204.

Cut an article out of the paper that pertains to their career or hobby and mail it to them with a short note.

205.

Send them a short e-mail reminding them of upcoming key birthdays and anniversaries of other members of your extended family. (They really do want to wish Uncle Bernie and Aunt Kathy a happy fortieth anniversary, but there's no way they'll remember it without you.)

206.

Buy and read a single issue of a specialty magazine that relates to their interest. (Especially if it's something they enjoy that you really don't understand.)

207.

Keep an open door. Be available.
Help first. Judge later.

208.

Ask if you can buy them lunch.

209.

If sometime they ask to buy you lunch, accept!

210.

Attend their sporting events. You went to all their games when they were younger. Games are less stressful and more enjoyable now. Parents rarely show up at college intramural games or park district men's softball. So, that makes your presence even more fun and surprising.

211.

Remind them about family gatherings, events, and traditions. Don't judge or be sarcastic if they don't make it.

212.

Keep the lines of communication flowing. If you haven't talked in six weeks, it gets more difficult to call. But if you have short conversations once or twice a week, you skip all the awkward small talk.

213.

Let them know they can still call you in an emergency.

214.

Talk to them like an adult. Talk about world
events. Tell them about what's going on in
your life. Treat them at least as well as you
treat a coworker. Respect their opinions.

215.

Be an attractive destination point. Make sure your
home is inviting and comfortable. Maintain the
traditions. Begin and end your time together with
smiles and hugs. With much laughter in between.

216.

Let them pick their own husband or wife.

217.

Be an awesome grandparent to your kids' kids.

Even More Saying
"I Love You" Every Day

218.

Start getting ready for church the night before, so that it's not a mad scramble in the morning and you arrive on time. (Scowling is not a proper way to begin your worship together!)

219.

Put their events on your work calendar.

220.

Listen with your eyes.

221.

Ask them, "If you had three wishes, what would you wish for?" (You'll start a fun conversation...and maybe get a peek at their hopes and dreams.)

222.

Spy on them. Know things about your kids that they don't know you know.

223.

Hang up some artwork or plaques that remind your entire family of who you are and what you stand for: "As for me and my house, we will serve the LORD" (Joshua 24:15 NKJV), "Through wisdom a house is built and by understanding it is established" (Proverbs 24:3 NKJV). Then live and lead your family in those truths.

224.

Turn them loose in a bookstore and let them each buy one book. (Not a CD or calendar or DVD.)

225.

Two words: Hershey's Kisses.

226.

Cuddle.

227.

Run your fingers through their hair.

228.

Give noogies.

229.

Be prepared for April Fool's Day. (As a joke crafter and a possible joke receiver. Help them learn the difference between mean jokes and clever jokes.)

230.

Teach them to make the sounds of disgusting bodily functions with their armpits. (They're going to learn it anyway, so they might as well learn it from you—along with teaching them when *not* to use that special talent.)

231.

Admit your mistakes.

232.

Embarrass them in front of their friends. (But not often.)

233.

Respect them. See them as future adults.

234.

Say things like "You can do anything you set your mind to" and "You have a great future ahead of you." But connect that prediction of future success to hard work and personal discipline. Especially as they get older, follow up lofty platitudes with action-oriented questions like, "What's your plan?" and "How can I help you achieve your dreams?" Here's the point: Your love is unconditional. But their success is very conditional.

235.

Make one of those origami fortune tellers (aka cootie catchers, chancers, or chatterboxes) and fill it with corny, uplifting words of encouragement.

236.

Explore a creek. Catch a tadpole.

237.

A recent survey indicated nearly three out of four
kids have never played hopscotch. Yikes! So…
teach your kids all those great games of your youth.
Hopscotch. Four Square. Kick the Can. Ghost
in the Graveyard. Spud. Freeze Tag. Red Rover.
Mother May I? Buck Buck. Capture the Flag.
Maybe even assemble a group of kids—and other
parents—to play until the streetlights come on.

238.

Know what they want. But give them what they need.

239.

Open up your high school yearbook on the kitchen
table and when they begin laughing at your hairstyle,
pledge to laugh at their high school yearbook 20 years
from now. (Admit that your high school hairstyle
would be completely embarrassing today and that it's
a good thing that hair can be grown out and restyled.
Then remind them that an embarrassing tattoo from
someone's youth cannot be changed quite as easily.)

240.

Clean their wounds with hydrogen peroxide, but don't say, "It won't hurt," because it might!

241.

When all the other parents give in, be the parent that says no.

242.

Coach their Little League team. Take the entire team to Dairy Queen after a disappointing loss.

243.

When they're eight years old and puking their guts out from the flu, gently hold their tummy and forehead and speak softly.

244.

If they're seventeen and puking their guts out from drinking, stand by the bathroom door, offer no sympathy, and make them clean it up. (Save the lecture for later.)

245.

Remember to lecture later. And follow through with appropriate punishment.

246.

Teeter-totter with them. Remember to move closer
to the middle to counterbalance their lighter weight.
Explain the physics of levers and fulcrums. (Warning:
you may not be able to find a seesaw anymore. Many
playgrounds only have "safe" equipment now!)

247.

Put down this silly book and go spend
five minutes with your kid.

248.

Dedicate something to them.

249.

Wear their photo on a button.

250.

Get some magnet letters for the fridge
and spell out nice things like "LUV U"
or "RYAN ROX" or "U R A QT."

251.

Hang out in their room.

Saying "I Love You"
Especially for Dads

252.
Give them whisker rubs.

253.
Send a Valentine to your daughter.

254.
Love their mother.

255.
Respect their mother. (No matter what!)

256.
Romance their mother. (Kiss
your wife in the kitchen.)

257.
Take your son to a Lamborghini dealership
and take a test drive together.

258.

Once a year listen to Harry Chapin's "Cat's in the Cradle" and Bob Carlisle's "Butterfly Kisses." Sing along. If your kids are in the room or the car with you, that's even better.

259.

For your next golfing foursome, ask your son or daughter to invite two friends. Pick up the greens fee.

260.

Quit golf. (Really. If it's interfering with you being a full-time dad, consider storing the clubs for a few years.)

261.

Take your daughter to the local park district "Daddy-Daughter Dance."

262.

Subscribe to *Sports Illustrated*. When the annual swimsuit edition comes, quietly take it out to the trash can.

263.

Teach them the right way to shake hands. Teach them to look the person they are meeting in the eye, smile, use their entire hands (not just the tips of the fingers), exert a firm but not crushing grip, and say, "Nice to meet you."

264.

When Mom says "Dinnertime," *immediately* turn off the TV, put the paper down, get off the computer, and go eat dinner.

265.

Let your preteen daughter and her friends style your hair in the silliest way possible. But only if they all agree to go out for pizza with you so you can show off your new coiffure.*

266.

Have a clean handkerchief ready, anytime and anyplace.

---

* Idea borrowed from speaker and author Josh McDowell.

Saying "I Love You" Especially for Moms

267.

Leave a big lipstick kiss on their cheek, forehead,
or on the back of their hand. If they groan,
roll their eyes, and wipe it off, that's okay.
You've made your point and they got it!

268.

Send a Valentine to each of your kids.

269.

Put notes in their lunch.

270.

Put small gifts in their lunch. Stickers, baseball
cards, puzzles, wind-up toys, or dime-
store junk that kids find so fascinating.

271.

In your big family purse, carry Band-Aids®, bug
spray, Chapstick®, and gum. (In your smaller
date purse, you can skip the bug spray.)

272.
Say good things about their father.

273.
Sometimes, do things that only
dads are supposed to do.

274.
Help your daughter know why it's critical to dress
modestly. Don't let her send the wrong signal to boys.

275.
Don't nag. Figure out your own personal
alternative to verbally nagging your kids: Make
lists. Leave sticky notes. Let some things
slide. Ask the kids to set their own deadlines.
Send sweet, non-nagging reminder texts.

276.

Make it a priority to have dinner as a family just about every night. Even if that means sometimes eating at 3:30 or 9:00 p.m.

277.

Whether you're a stay-at-home mom or a full-time employee, make sure your kids see the value in what you do and who you are as their mom.

278.

Post their "cutest" baby picture on Facebook.

Saying "I Love You"
in Difficult
Circumstances

279.

Allow them to experience the negative consequences of their bad decisions. Rescue them before there's any permanent damage.

280.

Decide now how you will respond to a phone call every parent dreads. "I wrecked the car." "I'm flunking out." "I'm at the police station." "I'm pregnant." "My girlfriend is pregnant." Recommended response: "I love you. It'll be okay. We'll get through this together."*

281.

Get wise counsel. From a pastor, elder, counselor, trusted physician, or older parent.

282.

Bring the family together. Circle the wagons. Lean on each other.

283.

Don't listen to gossip. Combat ignorance with truth.

---

* Idea borrowed from chapter 32, *52 Things Kids Need from a Dad.*

284.

Don't jump to conclusions about things that show up on Facebook. But as soon as possible, ask candidly about any troubling postings. Once it's out in the open, handle it with grace, truth, and the appropriate discipline.

285.

If they know they messed up, have confessed and asked forgiveness, don't pile it on. Reinforce the lesson. Bring closure. Move on.

286.

If you have legitimate cause…search their room, talk to school counselors, arrange for a drug test, and save their life.

287.

When any of your children begin a reckless slide down a slippery slope, intervene *before* they hit top speed and splatter at the bottom. That's true heroic parenting.

288.

Pray together. Even if they're not really
connected to God right now.

289.

Remember 1 Corinthians 13:4-8: "Love is patient,
love is kind. It does not envy, it does not boast, it is
not proud. It does not dishonor others, it is not self-
seeking, it is not easily angered, it keeps no record
of wrongs. Love does not delight in evil but rejoices
with the truth. It always protects, always trusts, always
hopes, always perseveres. Love never fails" (NIV).

Saying "I Love You" on Vacations

290.

Schedule some downtime. (Don't
come home exhausted and needing
a vacation from your vacation.)

291.

Don't make a big deal about sand in the car, stains
on the T-shirts, lost motel room keys, scratched
sunglasses, or misfolded maps. It's a vacation!

292.

Let the kids choose where to eat.

293.

Say no to any restaurant you've
already eaten at three times!

294.

Teach them to read a map.

295.

Teach them about Mapquest or GoogleMaps.

296.
Teach them about time zones.

297.
Teach them how to use a compass.

298.
Buy a travel guidebook and let them each choose
a sightseeing destination along the way.

299.
Keep the in-the-car movies to a minimum.

300.
Put them in charge of their own suitcase.

301.
Pull out a few surprise in-the-car games
on the third day of the trip.

302.
Sunscreen.

303.

Before checking out of any motel, make one last pass through the room. Hide the forgotten phone charger, sunglasses, headband, diary, retainer, baseball cap, or stuffed pony until one of the kids screams, "Stop! We have to go back." Then calmly produce the forgotten item. They'll never forget again.

304.

Find license plates from all 50 states. Beginning with "A" hunt for things beginning with every letter of the alphabet. Play "I Spy with My Little Eye." Count things like cows, windmills, water towers, 18-wheelers, VWs, barns, lonely trees, etc. Make it a contest between kids.

305.

Based on their gifts and abilities, give traveling assignments. Map reading and navigation. iPhone alerts for detours and traffic jams. Maintaining a wide assortment of CD and iPod tunes and audiobooks. Munchies management.

306.

Pull off the road, stretch your legs, and share a moment at historical markers or scenic views. (Read some of the plaques in a dramatic news anchor voice.)

307.

Anticipate getting on one another's nerves. Smile, because getting on one another's nerves is part of the trip!

308.

Visit some—but not all—of the classic vacation sites: Grand Canyon, Mount Rushmore, Kitty Hawk, Disney World, Niagara Falls, Everglades, Washington, DC, Wisconsin Dells, the Alamo, Yosemite, etc.

Activities That Say "I Love You"

(Even Though You Might Look Foolish and Your Kids Might Be Much Better Than You)

309.
Skateboarding

310.
Rock-climbing

311.
Kayaking

312.
Surfing

313.
Karaoke singing

314.
Going to a video game convention

315.
Parasailing

316.
Zip-lining

317.
Spelunking

318.
Dance Dance Revolution

Activities That Say "I Love You"

(At Which You Can Show Off Your Knowledge or Coolness)

319.

Take them to the Rock and Roll Hall of Fame
in Cleveland and finally make use of all that
knowledge about the lyrics, liner notes, and
lifestyle choices of the bands from your youth.

320.

Take them to your college campus and describe
the highs and lows of your academic career.

321.

Drive them around the neighborhood of your first
apartment. Remind them that you were young and
foolish once. Share a lesson you learned the hard way.

322.

Sign up for trivia contests sponsored by restaurants,
park districts, fundraisers, and social organizations.

323.

Instead of just dropping your kids off at church for youth group, Awana, Sunday school, or some other activity, stay and volunteer. Don't necessarily help lead your own child's age group or team. And don't be too cool. Just be yourself.

324.

Take your kids to your job site on an evening, weekend, or holiday when the place is virtually empty. Help them see your world. Introduce them to any security people, maintenance staff, or second-shift workers.

Still More Saying
"I Love You" Every Day

325.

Be sad when they're sad. (Sometimes the best way to cheer them up is to let them know how much you hurt for them.)*

326.

Be happy when they're happy. (Too often we rob their joy by pointing out future obstacles, missed opportunities, or upcoming obligations.)*

327.

Make job lists with little check-off boxes. (Don't rag or nag. Give deadlines and make sure they know your specific expectations.)

328.

Listen together to old comedy albums. Bill Cosby. Abbott & Costello. Burns & Allen. Steve Allen. Bob Newhart. Ponder what it must have been like before television was invented.

329.

Build a tree fort.

---

* Rejoice with those who rejoice, and weep with those who weep (Romans 12:15).

330.

At family-friendly restaurants, ask for an extra children's placemat so you can do twice as many mazes, puzzles, and connect-the-dot games!

331.

Make a heart-shaped cake. Here's how: Bake two small one-layer cakes. One in a round pan and one in a small square pan. Cut the round cake in half and arrange those two semi-circles on top of the square to a make a heart. Frost generously! Write your kids' names on it!

332.

Call your kids by name.

333.

Give them a positive, affirming nickname.

334.

Make up a cute little rhyme to say with their name.

335.

Make up a cute little song that repeats
their name a few times and includes the
word "love" or "my guy" or "my gal."

336.

You know how dating and married couples "have
a song"? Keep your ears open for just the right one
for each of your kids. It may include their name—
especially for girls. (e.g. "Michelle" by The Beatles,
"Rosanna" by Toto, "Mandy" by Barry Manilow,
"Barbara Ann" by The Beach Boys) Or substitute
their name for the name in the pop song. (e.g. sing
your daughter's name "Kaylee" in place of "Mandy,"
or sing "Samantha" instead of "Rosanna.")

337.

Two words: microwave popcorn.

338.

Let them see you praying. Often.

339.

Let them see you reading your Bible. Often.

340.

If you need to take an out-of-town trip for a few days, leave a box filled with invisible kisses, and make sure they grab one every time they think about you.

341.

Read bedtime stories. Do a voice for each character.

342.

Genuinely care about their friends.

343.

Start a file folder for each of your kids. When they proudly bring you a work of art, ask them to tell you all about it. Be awed by their creativity. Find something wonderful to admire. When they say, "You can keep it!" write their name and date on it…and slip it in the file folder.*

344.

Frame one of their more thought-provoking and creative works of art.*

345.

Make sure they can trust you. Keep your word. Keep their secrets.

---

* Idea borrowed from chapter 5, *52 Things Kids Need from a Dad*.

346.

Take them to a professional baseball game and teach them how to keep score. I recommend Wrigley Field.

347.

Put up a basketball hoop in the driveway. Play H-O-R-S-E. Do not let them beat you. (They'll know if you're not trying your hardest and besides they will emerge victorious on their own soon enough!)

348.

If they do beat you, insist that you meant to play H-O-R-S-E-F-L-Y.

Saying "I Love You" During the Holidays

349.

Assign decorating jobs. (And don't ridicule the lopsided lighting or mismatched bunting.)

350.

Go ahead and send out one of those corny, boastful, over-the-top Christmas Brag Letters to everyone on your Christmas list and put an ultra-positive spin on every event, accomplishment, and milestone from the entire year. (Anyone who scoffs or rolls their eyes is just jealous of your amazing kids!)

351.

Light lots of candles. See their eyes sparkle.

352.

Let them light the candles. (Cool!)

353.

Let them blow out the candles. (Even cooler!)

354.

Assign one child to say grace before the big family meal. (Give them advance notice.)

355.

Include the little ones in the toasting and clinking of glasses.

356.

On behalf of each of your own kids, sponsor a Christmas gift for the child of an inmate through Angel Tree with Prison Fellowship.

357.

Explore ethnic and cultural traditions. Tell them about your long-ago family traditions. And bring your favorite ones back.

358.

Take your younger children out one at a time to buy gifts for your spouse and their siblings. (Have them make a list first.)

359.

Invite friends of your children to join your festivities. Especially kids who are going through something difficult at home. Or students from out of town who can't get home for the holiday.

360.

Let them stay up until midnight with you on New Year's Eve. (That's much more memorable for you than any booze-filled gathering of strangers in a hotel banquet hall.)

Saying "I Love You" for Life

361.

There are a handful of critical turning points in every child's life when they really need their mom and dad. To share the joy. Or lift a burden. Be there.

362.

Enter their world. Invite them into your world. Discover points of connection. Seek to understand each other.

363.

With just about every interaction, you can push your kids away or draw them closer to you. Choose to break down barriers, open doors, and build bridges.

364.

Seek, find, and worship God together.

365.

Just speak it. Say "I love you so much."

To learn more about other books by Jay Payleitner
and to read sample chapters, log on to our website:

www.harvesthousepublishers.com

HARVEST HOUSE PUBLISHERS
EUGENE, OREGON